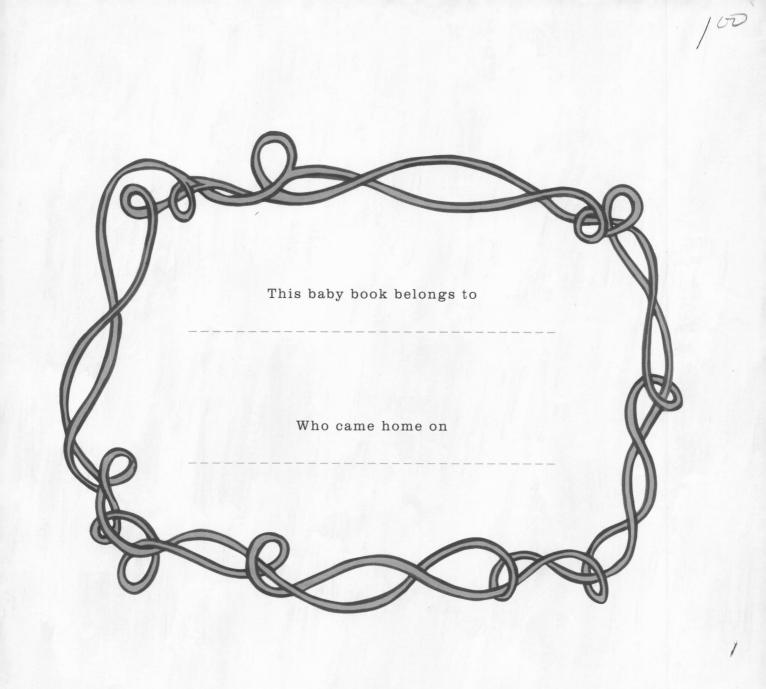

This baby book belongs to

_____

Who came home on

_____

Text by Zoe Francesca
Illustrations by Susie Ghahremani / boygirlparty.com
Design by Jennifer Muller at Lucky Tangerine

Typeset in Clarendon, Fling & Kursivschrift Steh Har
Manufactured in China

Chronicle Books endeavors to use environmentally
responsible paper in its gift and stationery products.

10 9 8 7 6 5

Chronicle Books LLC
680 Second Street
San Francisco, CA 94107
www.chroniclebooks.com

My Family, My Journey

CHRONICLE BOOKS
680 SECOND STREET
SAN FRANCISCO, CA 94107
WWW.CHRONICLEBOOKS.COM

paste family photograph here

Our family photo before you came to us

day   month   year

Before You Were Born

The story of us and how we came to be a family

paste family photograph here.

Our first family photo with you

day　　　　　month　　　　　year

The Story of Your Adoption

Why we chose to adopt

How we found you

Our hopes and dreams for you

People Who
Helped Us Find You

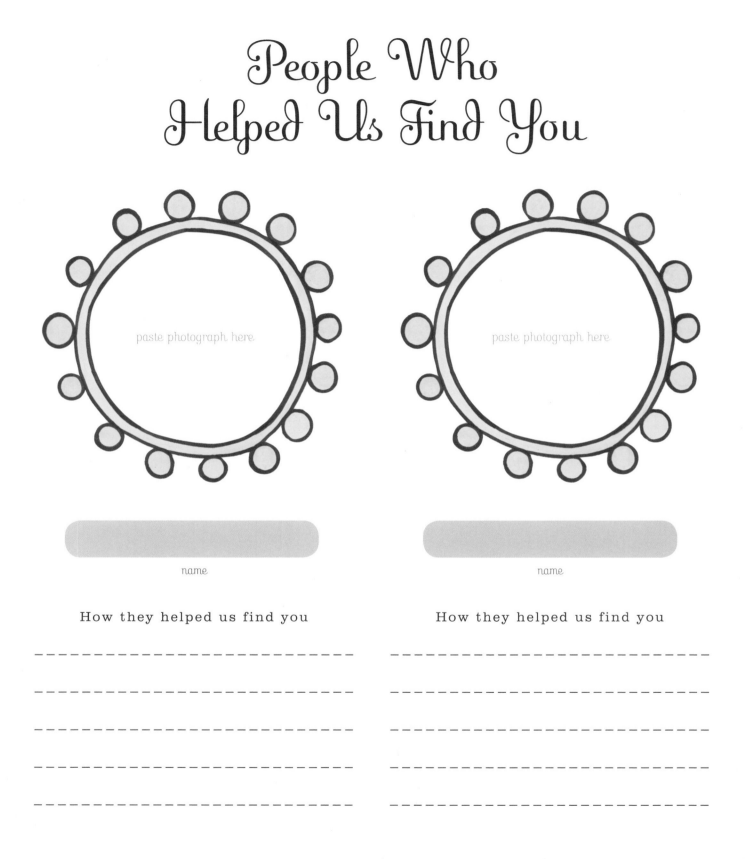

paste photograph here

paste photograph here

name

name

How they helped us find you

How they helped us find you

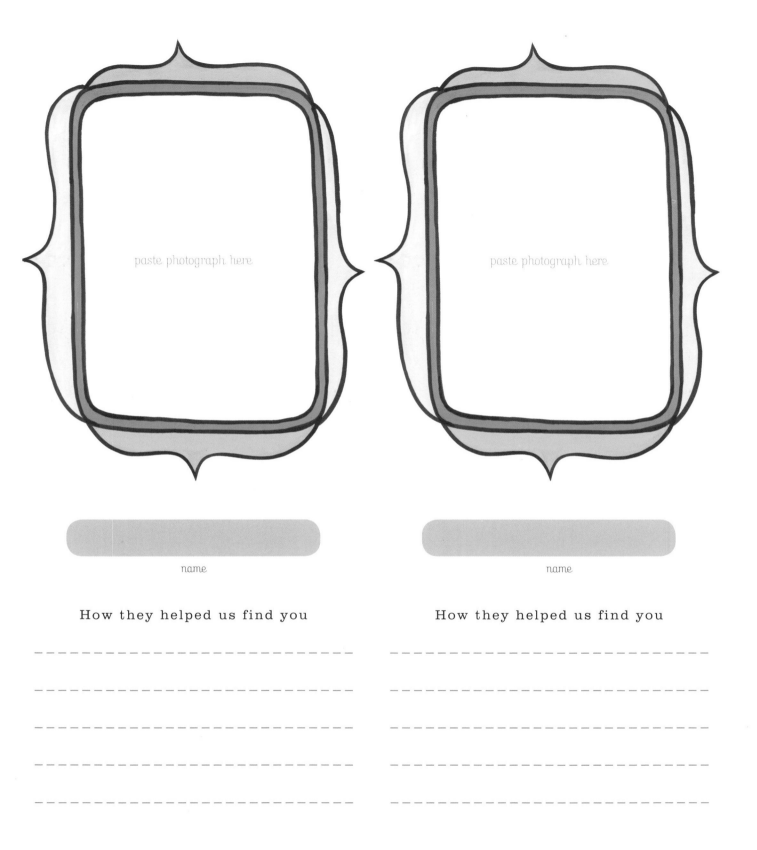

paste photograph here

paste photograph here

name

name

How they helped us find you

How they helped us find you

Waiting

Plans and preparations we made

_____

_____

_____

_____

_____

_____

The Match!

We were matched to you on

day   month   year

How we found out

How we celebrated

A Baby Shower!

paste shower invitation here

Favorite Shower Memories

Special Guests

Special Gifts

Our Journey To You

Where you were

How we got to you

Joyful memories

paste family photograph here

Our Very First Meeting

Our first impression of you

Your first impression of us

All About Your Name

name

Why we chose your name

What it means and where it came from

----

nickname

All About Your Birthday

Your birthday is

day   month   year

Your astrological sign is

What we know about your birthdate

Our Family

Just some of the people who love you

Name

Relationship

favorite food

favorite color

favorite animal

Name

Relationship

----

favorite food

favorite color

favorite animal

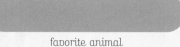

Name

- -

Relationship

- -

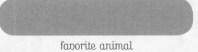

favorite food

favorite color

favorite animal

- -

- -

- -

- -

Name

- -

Relationship

- -

favorite food

favorite color

favorite animal

- -

- -

- -

- -

welcome home

Coming Home

You came home on

| day | month | year |

Your trip home

You wore

Your New Home

paste in photograph of baby's room.

Baby's room!

What you thought of your new home

What we did on your first day home

Introductions & Celebrations

Some of the first people you met

Favorite stories

Favorite presents

----------------------------   ----------------------------

----------------------------   ----------------------------

----------------------------   ----------------------------

----------------------------   ----------------------------

Your Announcement

paste in photograph

We sent out your announcement on

day   month   year

Your Adoption Buddies

paste photograph here

paste photograph here

child's name

child's name

parents' names

parents' names

Favorite memories

Favorite memories

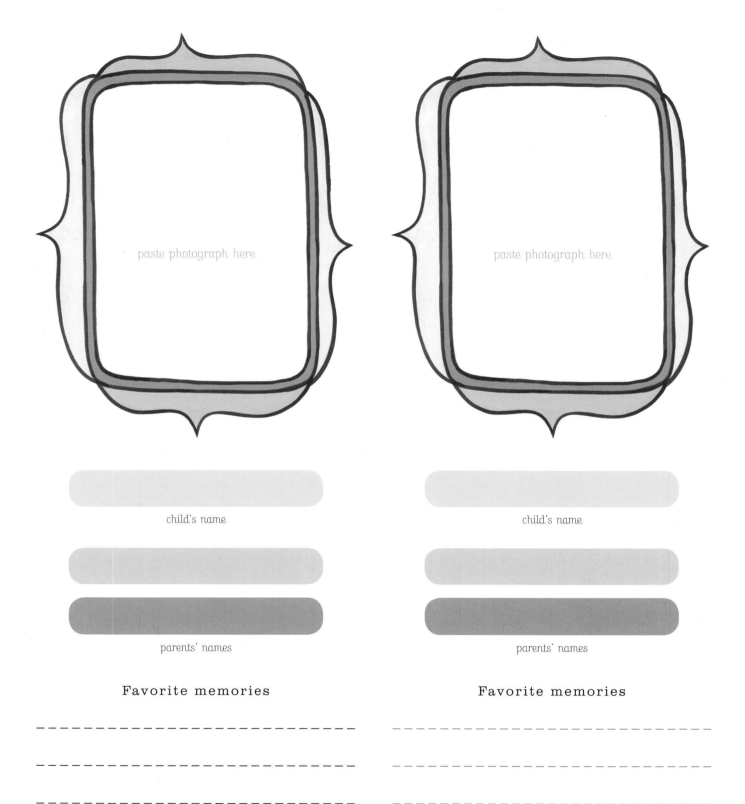

paste photograph here

paste photograph here

child's name

child's name

parents' names

parents' names

Favorite memories

Favorite memories

Your First Year With Us

month
1

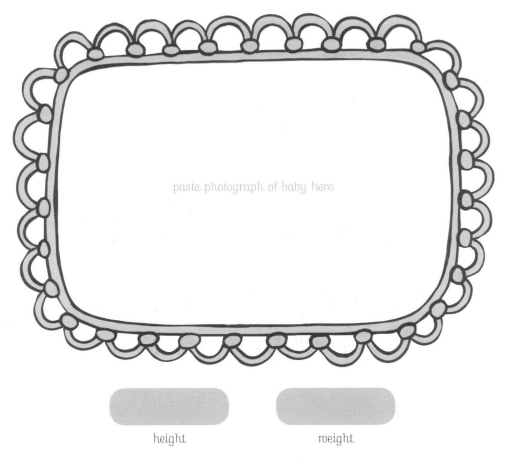

paste photograph of baby here

height   weight

Memorable Moments & Milestones

month
2

paste photograph of baby here

height

weight

Memorable Moments & Milestones

- -

- -

- -

- -

month
3

paste photograph of baby here

height   weight

Memorable Moments & Milestones

month
4

paste photograph of baby here

height

weight

Memorable Moments & Milestones

month
5

paste photograph of baby here

height

weight

Memorable Moments & Milestones

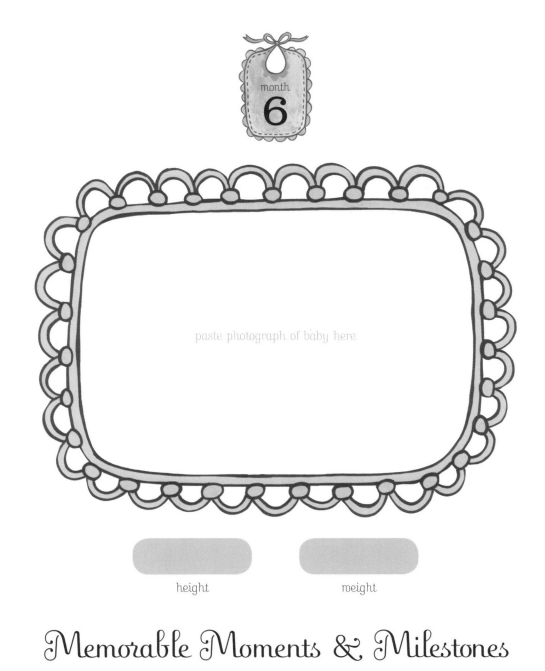

month
6

paste photograph of baby here

height   weight

Memorable Moments & Milestones

month
7

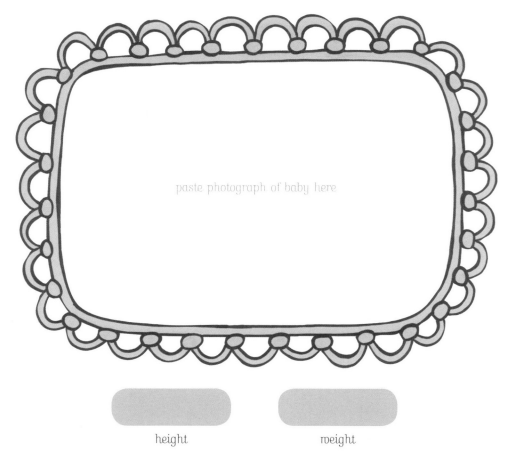

paste photograph of baby here

height   weight

Memorable Moments & Milestones

_____

_____

_____

_____

month

8

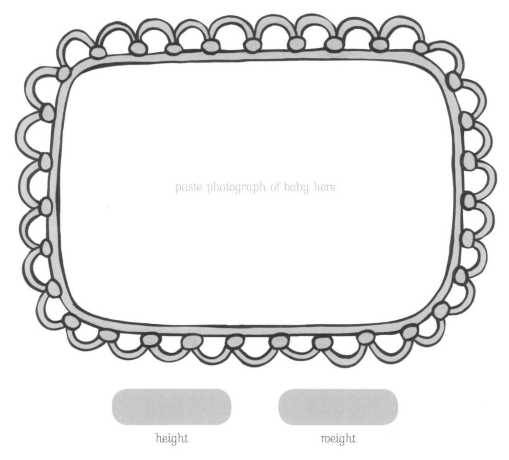

paste photograph of baby here

height   weight

Memorable Moments & Milestones

month
9

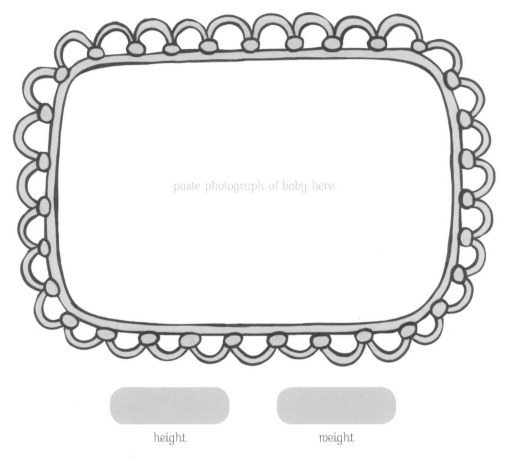

paste photograph of baby here

height   weight

Memorable Moments & Milestones

_____

_____

_____

_____

month
10

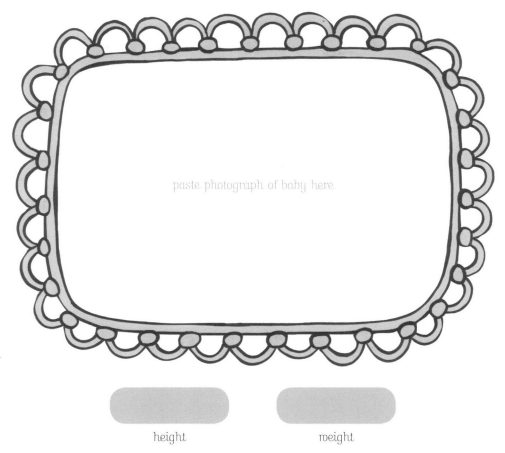

paste photograph of baby here

height   weight

Memorable Moments & Milestones

month
11

paste photograph of baby here

height   weight

Memorable Moments & Milestones

month
12

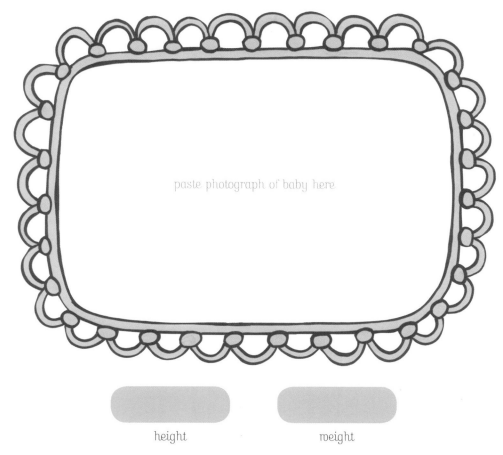

paste photograph of baby here

height   weight

Memorable Moments & Milestones

Firsts and Favorites

First word

- -

Favorite toys

- - - - - - - - - - - - - - - - - -   - - - - - - - - - - - - - - - - - - -

- - - - - - - - - - - - - - - - - -   - - - - - - - - - - - - - - - - - - -

- - - - - - - - - - - - - - - - - -   - - - - - - - - - - - - - - - - - - -

- - - - - - - - - - - - - - - - - -   - - - - - - - - - - - - - - - - - - -

First night you slept all the way through

day   month   year

Favorite foods

- - - - - - - - - - - - - - - - - -   - - - - - - - - - - - - - - - - - - -

- - - - - - - - - - - - - - - - - -   - - - - - - - - - - - - - - - - - - -

- - - - - - - - - - - - - - - - - -   - - - - - - - - - - - - - - - - - - -

- - - - - - - - - - - - - - - - - -   - - - - - - - - - - - - - - - - - - -

First step

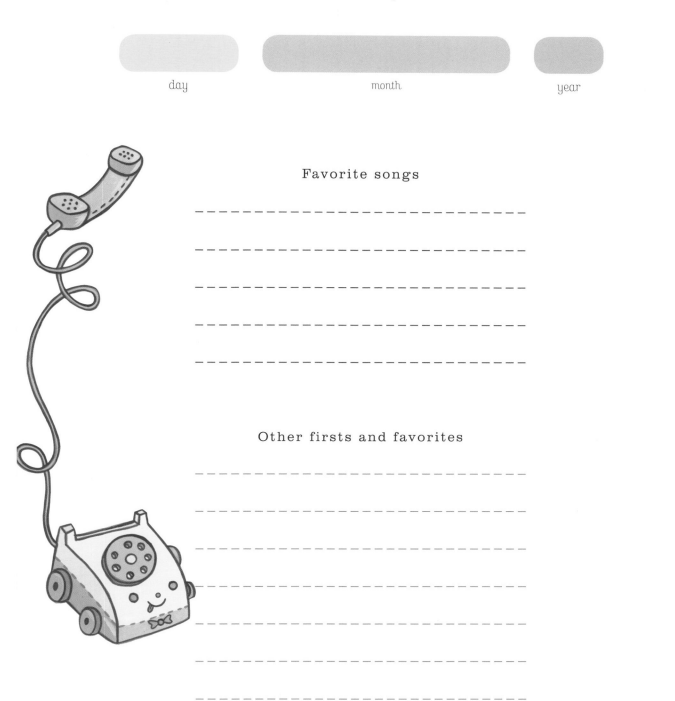

day   month   year

Favorite songs

_____

_____

_____

_____

_____

Other firsts and favorites

_____

_____

_____

_____

_____

_____

_____

Your Adoption Day

Your adoption day is

day   month   year

The judge's name is

- -

The special people who were there

How we celebrated

- -

- -

- -

paste adoption day photograph here

You, on your adoption day

Your First Birthday With Us

On your birthday, you wore

- -

All about your birthday cake

- -

The special people who attended

- - - - - - - - - - - - -   - - - - - - - - - - - - -   - - - - - - - - - - - - -

- - - - - - - - - - - - -   - - - - - - - - - - - - -   - - - - - - - - - - - - -

Gifts you received

- - - - - - - - - -   - - - - - - - - - -

- - - - - - - - - -   - - - - - - - - - -   - - - - - - - - - -

paste birthday photographs here

Happy Birthday!

Things That
Make You Smile

Things That
Make You Cry

What We Know About Your Birth Family and Where You Came From

Paste leaf stickers (located in the pocket at the back of the book) on the branches to create family trees.

Notes

Notes